CONTENTS

Camel fair, p.35

INTRODUCING INDIA

What's hot: India	6
India facts and stats	8
People	10
Six stereotypes	12

CITIES AND TRANSPORT

Whirlwind tour of Mumbai	14
Getting around	16

SHOPPING

Visiting the bazaar	18

FOOD

Regional food	20
India – snack heaven	22

FILM AND MUSIC

Bollywood!	24
Music in India	26
Music festivals	28

SPORT AND LEISURE

Adventure sports	30
India – a cricket-crazy country	32
Free time	34

RELIGION

Religious sites and festivals	36

FRINGES OF INDIA

The Himalayas	38
Offshore islands	40

THE ESSENTIALS

Key information for travellers	42
Finding out more	45
Index	46

WHAT'S HOT: INDIA

Lakshadweep islands, p.40

There are so many things to see and do in India that it's hard to know where to start. Should you go to the high mountains, raft down a river, visit a big city or a tropical beach? Do you want to see ancient palaces, listen to music or haggle in a bazaar? Perhaps this list will give you some ideas.

1. CATCH THE SUNSET ON A MUMBAI BEACH pp.14–15

On a clear evening, join the crowds of locals enjoying sunset over the Indian Ocean. (And if you're feeling hungry afterwards, there's a guide to some of Mumbai's best snacks on page 22.)

2. RIDE IN AN AUTO-RICKSHAW p.16

These little three-wheeled vehicles are like a motor scooter that's mated with a giant wheelbarrow, with a roof on top. Riding one through a busy Indian city can be a bit like going on a rollercoaster: you won't know how scary it is until it's too late to get off.

3. SPEND THE EVENING AT A BOLLYWOOD MOVIE p.24

There are cinemas in most towns and cities and mobile screenings in rural areas. Brush up on your Hinglish before you go, though. Use the beginner's guide on page 25.

4. GO TO SLEEP LISTENING TO LIVE MUSIC p.28

If you camp at the Storm Music Festival in Coorg, you'll find that after the official show has finished, the musicians often come out and play around the campfires.

THE
REAL
INDIA

Your need-to-know guide
for all things Indian

Sunny Chopra

First published in 2014
by Franklin Watts

Copyright © Franklin Watts 2014

Franklin Watts
338 Euston Road
London NW1 3BH

Franklin Watts Australia
Level 17/207 Kent Street
Sydney, NSW 2000

All rights reserved.

Series editor: Sarah Peutrill
Series designer: Sophie Wilkins
Picture researcher: Diana Morris

Dewey number: 954'.0532
HB ISBN: 978 1 4451 1974 8
Library ebook ISBN: 978 1 4451 2803 0

Printed in Malaysia

Franklin Watts is a division of Hachette
Children's Books, an Hachette UK company.
www.hachette.co.uk

INTRODUCING INDIA

Cricket, p. 32

5. TAKE IN A CRICKET MATCH p.32

Indians are big sports fans, and the sport they love most of all is cricket. Going to a match at any of the big grounds is a lively experience. There's a guide to the best ones on page 33.

6. SPEND THE DAY COVERED IN COLOURED POWDER AND WATER p.37

Holi is one of the biggest religious festivals in India. Don't expect to sit quietly praying though – instead, people spend the day drenching each other with water and throwing coloured powder.

7. TREK THROUGH A HIDDEN HIMALAYAN VALLEY p.38

This could be a good antidote if you get tired of the hustle and bustle of Indian life. Up in the high mountains are valleys with no cars and hardly any people.

IT'S (NEARLY) OFFICIAL!
TOP PLACES TO VISIT IN INDIA

Members of one of the world's biggest travel websites picked these top Indian cities to visit:

1. New Delhi – the capital city combines modern design, ancient buildings and monuments, and grand avenues and parks.

2. Jaipur – the bazaars, palaces and forts make 'the pink city' one of the most beautiful places to visit in India.

3. Goa – Indian, Portuguese and hippie cultures combine here, making Goa a top pick for those who like music and sunshine.

4. Mumbai – famous for its chaotic streets, outdoor bazaars, food and beautiful beach sunsets.

5. Agra – the site of India's most famous building, the Taj Mahal. Built by the Emperor Shah Jahan in memory of his beloved wife, the Taj Mahal is still drawing crowds 350 years later.

6. Varanasi – visitors and Indians alike come here because of the River Ganges. The pilgrims come to bathe in the holy water and to worship at the many beautiful temples.

7. Bangalore (Bengaluru) – known as a centre for India's hi-tech industries, Bangalore is called the Garden City because of its beautiful gardens, palaces and lakes.

INDIA
FACTS AND STATS

India makes your head spin. There are beautiful beaches, breathtaking mountains and wonderful ancient temples. On the way to see them, you pass slums where hundreds of people share one water tap. India is a land of staggering contrasts.

Many farmers still use oxen to pull their ploughs

LANDSCAPE

In the far north, the world's highest mountains attract climbers and trekkers from all around the world. Many are heading for Kanchenjunga, India's highest mountain and the third-tallest on Earth. South of the Himalayas are flat lands where the Indus, Ganges and Brahmaputra rivers flow. To the west is the Thar Desert. And further south again are areas of high, flat land broken by hills. On the east and west coasts of India are flat plains, with thousands of kilometres of beautiful beaches and warm seas.

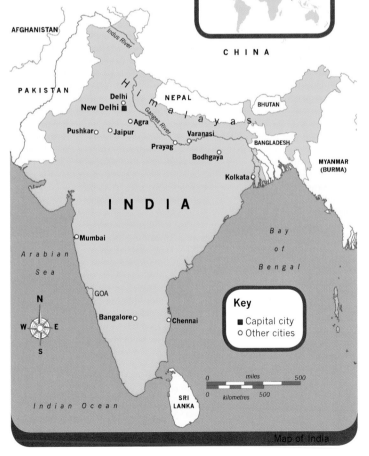

Map of India

Key
■ Capital city
○ Other cities

CLIMATE

India's climate may come as a bit of a shock. During summer, from March to May, it can be uncomfortably hot and sweaty. The coast is cooler, but sweatier. Only the highest hills and mountains are comfortable.

Between June and September heavy monsoon rains arrive. An umbrella is essential travelling gear! Sudden floods are a danger during the monsoon.

In winter (January and February) temperatures fall. The days are warm, but the nights can be chilly. In some places the temperature drops below freezing.

INDIA AND PAKISTAN

India and neighbouring Pakistan are bitter rivals. The two countries were formed one day apart, in 1947. Ever since, they have been arguing over territory. The argument is fiercest in the northern mountains. Here, some areas are restricted to visitors and army checkpoints are common.

"There are some parts of the world that, once visited, get into your heart and won't go. For me, India is such a place."

— Keith Bellows, National Geographic Society

FACT FILE ONE

CAPITAL CITY: New Delhi

AREA: 2,973,193 km² (land territory), plus 314,070 km² (ocean territory)

HIGHEST MOUNTAIN: Kanchenjunga, eastern Himalayas (8,598 m)

LOWEST POINT: Indian Ocean (0 m)

LONGEST RIVER: Ganges (2,525 km)

BORDERS: Bangladesh, Bhutan, Burma (Republic of Myanmar), China, Nepal, Pakistan

NATURAL HAZARDS: droughts, flooding, earthquakes

A climber in the Himalayas

PEOPLE

India has over 2,000 different ethnic groups and hundreds of languages. However, most people (four in every five Indians) follow the Hindu religion. The bright colours, ceremonies and sometimes riotous festivals of Hinduism unite people throughout the country.

Hindus celebrate the festival of Holi, see p.37

"India has two million gods, and worships them all. In religion all other countries are paupers; only India is a millionaire."

— Mark Twain, American writer

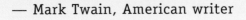
Different castes mix more freely in urban areas than in the countryside

THE CASTE SYSTEM

Hinduism puts people into four castes. Caste determines your work, who you marry, where you live and more. The castes are: Brahmins, or priests; Kshatriyas, warriors and rulers; Vaishyas, merchants and minor officials; and Sudras, who do unskilled work. Those with no caste are known as Dalits, Harijans or Untouchables.

In the cities, caste is slowly becoming less important. Modern Indian companies are more interested in whether their employees understand computers than which caste they are from. In the countryside though, the caste system is still strong.

RICH AND POOR

Although India is an increasingly wealthy country, many Indians are very poor. The poor live in crowded, low-quality housing, without running water or electricity. The poorest children may not go to school – especially girls, who instead are taught cooking and other household jobs at home.

Because of the poverty some Indians live in, and the wealth of some visitors, crime against rimes against travellers can happen: the money and possessions travellers carry are a small fortune to a poor Indian. Because of this, it is a good idea to stay in well-lit, busy areas, and avoid showing off cameras, electronic devices and large amounts of money.

A poverty-stricken family outside their home in New Delhi.

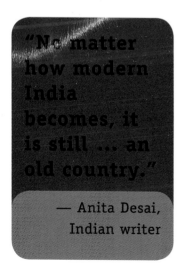
"No matter how modern India becomes, it is still ... an old country."

— Anita Desai, Indian writer

FACT FILE TWO

POPULATION: 1.2 billion

MAJOR CITIES: New Delhi (22 million), Mumbai (19 million), Kolkata (15 million), Chennai (7 million), Bangalore (7 million)

AGE STRUCTURE: 28.9% under 15 years old; 65.5% 15–64 years old; 5.7% over 64 years old

YOUTH UNEMPLOYMENT (15–24 year-olds): 10.2%

OBESITY: 1.9%

LANGUAGES: India has 15 official languages. Hindi is spoken by 41% of people; the rest speak Bengali, Telugu, Marathi, Tamil, Urdu, Gujurati or other Indian languages. English is often used as a second language.

RELIGIONS: Hinduism (80.5%), Islam (13.4%), Christianity (2.3%), Sikhism (1.9%)

SIX STEREOTYPES

Many travellers arrive in India with an idea of what the country is like already fixed in their minds. They are in for a shock! India probably won't be at all as they imagine. Before visiting, have a look at these six stereotypes. Are they true – or false?

Stereotype 1: Most Indians lack education

Even the poorest people usually try to make sure their children go to school. School itself is very demanding, and many students have extra lessons once proper school has finished.

Verdict: False!

Stereotype 2: There are cows everywhere

Most Indians are Hindus and for Hindus cows are sacred animals. They are allowed to wander freely around – not only in the countryside, but also in towns and cities.

Verdict: This one's true

Stereotype 3: There are also snake charmers everywhere

Snake charming is an ancient profession, handed down from father to son. But you see far fewer snake charmers than in the past – probably because it has been illegal since the 1990s.

Verdict: False!

Stereotype 4: All of India is dirty and chaotic

If you're looking for dirt and chaos, you can find it in India – alongside luxury hotels, glass-and-marble shopping malls, smart cafés and restaurants.

Verdict: False!

MATTU PONGAL – THE COW-PROSPERITY FESTIVAL

In southern India, Mattu Pongal is held at harvest time. *Mattu* is the local word for 'cow', and *pongal* stands for 'prosperity'. In the evening, young men chase bulls through the streets, trying to pick off the money attached to their horns.

Skyline of Mumbai, one of India's biggest cities

Stereotype 5: People only eat curry

'Curry' is an English version of the southern-Indian word *kari*, a meal of spiced vegetables or meat. The English decided to use 'curry' to describe ALL Indian cooking. In fact, every region of India has its own style of cooking.

Verdict: Not even an Indian word – False!

Stereotype 6: Indians are poor

There ARE a lot of poor people in India (though even the poor seem to smile a lot). But India is also home to some of the world's richest people. And a large number of Indians have good jobs and live in nice homes.

Verdict: False!

There is a wealthy Indian middle class, who own the usual gadgets

WHIRLWIND TOUR OF MUMBAI

Washing clothes, Dhobi Ghat

Mumbai is India's second-biggest city, and it's where many visitors arrive. Before you head off to the Indian Ocean beaches or the high mountains, why not take a whirlwind tour of the bits of Mumbai most travellers don't visit?

09:00 hours – Stop 1: Mahalaxmi Dhobi Ghat

Each day, dirty washing is brought here from all over the city. You'll never forget the noise and the bright colours of the drying clothes. Take a moment to wonder how the right clothes get back to their owners...

11:30–12:30 – Stop 2: Churchgate Station

Each day, around 200,000 lunch boxes are delivered by Mumbai's *dabbawala* (lunchbox carriers). Churchgate Station is a great place to watch them set off with tin boxes, piled-high trays balanced on their heads.

15:00–16:00 – Stop 3: Chor Bazaar (Thieves' Market)

Watch out for pickpockets! On Fridays, Chor Bazaar is crammed with stalls selling all kinds of goodies – many of them said to be stolen. Of course, there are plenty of honest purchases you can make!

1800 – Stop 4: Marine Drive Beach

A great place to relax and have a cool drink, alongside the local people who come here to watch the sunset.

Mumbai looks out on the Arabian Sea, and is famous for its beautiful sunsets

OTHER TOP INDIAN CITIES TO VISIT

Among the hundreds of amazing cities you could visit, these are some of the top picks:

1. New Delhi – This modern, architect-designed city was built on the remains of seven ancient Indian cities, so there are reminders of India's past all around.

2. Kolkata – From the old English graveyard at South Park Street Cemetery, to the ultra-modern Science City, Kolkata has lots to do. Take a tram from Esplanade along the racecourse route to see many of the key sights.

3. Udaipur – This city is sometimes nicknamed City of Lakes, because it grew up around a series of beautiful lakes. It is famous for its breathtaking palaces – Udaipur is a great place for imagining what it would have been like to be a rajah (ruler) centuries ago!

4. Hampi – Now a village, but once capital of a great Hindu kingdom, Hampi is famous for ruins that date back to the 1300s.

Hindus celebrate the Holi festival at the ancient ruined city of Hampi

GETTING AROUND

An old goods train in front of a waterfall, Goa

India is a huge country. Most foreign visitors arrive by plane – but once you're there, what are the best ways to get around? It depends a lot on how far you're going and whether you are in the city or the countryside.

AUTO-RICKSHAWS

For travellers, probably the most fun way to get around India's cities is by auto-rickshaw. These are little three-wheeled taxis, with a seat in front for the driver and a bench behind for passengers*. They snake through crowded streets far more easily than a car. Auto-rickshaws aren't great for longer journeys, because the sides are open to pollution and dust. For a short trip, though, they are ideal.

*Make sure your bags are on the inside! The sides are open, and thieves on scooters have been known to reach in and grab people's bags.

TIPS FOR A HAPPY RICKSHAW RIDE

1. Try to pick a new-ish looking rickshaw, with seats in good condition.

2. Young drivers playing blaring music will probably offer a more exciting passenger experience, if that's what you want.

3. If the meter looks like it has been tampered with, pick a different rickshaw.

TRAINS

For long journeys, trains are a great way to travel.* Travelling by train is one of the highlights of visiting India. Book a seat in an air-conditioned carriage: it's more comfortable, and you can use the 'retiring room' at the station to wait for the train! Once aboard, these carriages usually have a dining service.

*Train trivia: Indian Railways is said to employ 1.6 million people, making it the world's second-largest employer.

Travelling to Chennai in comfort by train

METRO TRAINS

Some Indian cities have modern metro trains, which can be a great way to get around. Most trains have special women-only carriages, helping female travellers feel safer. Bangalore, Delhi, Jaipur and Kolkata already have modern metro systems, but the government plans that all Indian cities of more than two million people will have a metro by 2020.

Crowded metro carriage, New Delhi

THE INDRAIL PASS

If you're making a long visit to India, buy an Indrail pass before you get there. It lets you travel anywhere on Indian Railways for 90 days. All you have to do is reserve a seat.

BUSES

Sitting on the roof for a better view is no longer allowed, but riding the bus is still dangerous. Buses are often very full, the drivers may go dangerously fast, and thefts and attacks on travellers sometimes happen. Night buses are definitely best avoided.

VISITING THE BAZAAR

Bazaars, or markets, are an important part of life in India. They are where many Indians get their food, clothes and other goods. Wandering round an Indian bazaar can be slightly bewildering at first. Even so, most visitors end up feeling it was an unforgettable experience.

Chandni Chowk, Old Delhi

HOW TO HAGGLE

If you fancy haggling just like a local in the bazaar, here are a few tactics:

- Look shocked when you hear the price.
- If you're a good actor, try looking embarrassed for the seller. "Why so much. They're half that price down the road."
- Name a price you'd be willing to pay... which is half what you REALLY want to pay.
- Be prepared to go back and forth several times, with both you and the seller pretending to be shocked, horrified and upset, before finally agreeing a price.

INDIA'S MOST FAMOUS BAZAAR

If you're visiting a bazaar, why not make it one of the most famous? Chandni Chowk in Delhi is one of the biggest, oldest and busiest markets in India. It was built by Shah Jahan, Emperor of India in the 1600s.

The market runs through the heart of Old Delhi. Off the main streets you see crowded, crumbling old alleyways. They are filled with stalls where you can buy all kinds of typical Indian goods: sweets, snacks, clothes, books, shoes and lots more.

OTHER GREAT INDIAN BAZAARS

1. Chennai – "This is not for the weak-hearted", said one traveller, "It is very chaotic." All kinds of goods, very cheap, but also VERY busy and crowded.

2. Jaipur – In a city famous for bazaars, Johari bazaar is worth an early-morning visit (from 7 a.m.) to see the fruit, vegetable and flower sellers starting their day.

3. Kolkata – New Market (also called Hogg's Market) is the oldest bazaar in the city. There are over 2,000 stalls, plus in the evening thousands of street sellers on the pavements.

4. Mumbai – Colaba Causeway bazaar is aimed at travellers. Indians say *Sab kuch milega*, meaning, 'You'll get everything'. As one of the things you can get is your name written on a grain of rice, it's probably true.

A Jaipur bazaar

SHOPPING

5. Shimla – It gets cold up here in northern India – which might be why The Mall bazaar is famous for its woollen hats, sweaters, gloves and scarves.

Jewellery can be found in most bazaars

REGIONAL FOOD

Indians take food seriously. Eating together is an important part of family life, and cooks take great pride in their recipes. Dishes are almost always spiced to make them smell and taste better. Apart from that, though, what people eat varies from place to place.

Cooking lunch – several different dishes

WHEN (AND WHAT) PEOPLE EAT

The main meal of the day in India is usually either lunch or dinner. Traditionally, anyone who can afford it will eat four meals a day:

08:00: Breakfast (tea or coffee, often followed by toast or some sort of bread)

13:00: Lunch

16:00: A mid-afternoon snack, sometimes called 'tiffin'

21:00: Evening meal

What people eat depends on where they live. See the map opposite for more information.

WOMEN IN THE KITCHEN

Women do most of the cooking, and recipes and techniques are passed from mother to daughter. They often make every ingredient, even down to grinding their own flour. Most meals include several dishes: rice, bread, meat, vegetables and a sweet dessert.

FOOD WISDOM

Lots of Indian sayings feature food – here are two:

There's something black in the lentils – Something's wrong here.

Does a monkey enjoy ginger? – Someone is too stupid to understand.

NORTH

Northern food often has a thick, creamy sauce and is not too spicy-hot. Expect to eat lots of different vegetables and to find fruit in many dishes. Bread is more popular than rice.

Typical dish: *Mutter paneer*, curry made with home-made cheese and peas

Delhi
New Delhi
Pushkar
Agra
Jaipur
Varanasi
Prayag
Bodhgaya
Kolkata

WEST

Visitors to western India are spoilt for choice, as the food here is very diverse. It is mainly vegetarian, and some curries are spicy, others sweeter. On the coast people add coconut and chillies.

Typical dish: *Thaali*, or 'large plate', with up to 10 different vegetable dishes, bread, rice and sweets

Mumbai

EAST

Food here is simple, using fresh ingredients. Rice is a popular basic food, but green vegetables and fruit are often used too. East Indians are famous for loving sweets!

Typical dish: *Momos*, steamed dumplings filled with meat or vegetables

GOA
Bangalore
Chennai

SOUTH

Southern India is the place to visit if you like spicy-hot food. Few dishes use meat, though in coastal areas seafood curries are common. Rice is the basic part of many meals.

Typical dish: *Sambar*, spicy vegetable stew

Food map of India

FOOD

INDIA – SNACK HEAVEN

Mocambo Cafe in Fort, Mumbai

Nowhere does snack food quite like India. In cities, you're never far from somewhere to get a little bite to eat. Indian snack food is amazingly varied. It's also mouthwatering: we challenge you to read this selection of snacks without feeling at least a LITTLE bit hungry.

MUMBAI – SNACKING HEAVEN

Mumbai is India's second-biggest city. People move here from all over the country, bringing their tastes in food with them. This makes Mumbai a great place to try some of India's best snack food. Here are five local favourites to look out for:

1. Pav bhaji: a spicy vegetable sauce with a slab of butter, plus fluffy rolls and ... more butter.

2 Kebabs: Hindus don't eat beef, but in Muslim areas you can get beef kebabs. They'll be crisp on the outside, moist on the inside and taste slightly of mint. Yum!

Kebabs

3. Vada pav: potato cakes mashed with garlic, chili and coriander, dipped in chickpea batter, deep fried and served in a buttered white roll with coriander chutney.

4. Pani puri: Take a fried ball of batter filled with potato, onion, chickpeas and lentils. Dip it in an Indian version of sweet-and-sour sauce, then dip it in a coriander and mint sauce, and then eat.

Pani puri

5. Keema pav: carnivorous breakfast, Mumbai style. It's a plate of fried, spiced lamb mince, served with bread for mopping up the juice.

LASSI

Lassi is a cool drink that is great with India's spicy dishes. It's a mixture of yoghurt, water and other flavours such as fruit. Don't buy it from street sellers: it may not be hygienic.

TIPS FOR HAPPY SNACKING

Most visitors to India get an upset stomach. Being scared to move more than two metres from a toilet can easily spoil your holiday – but these tips will help you avoid tummy trouble:

1. Buy food from busy restaurants, where it will be fresher;

2. Avoid places that don't look clean, where you can't see the kitchen or where food has been standing in the open air;

3. Don't eat sliced fruit, salads or anything else that might have been washed in water – buy hot cooked food.

FOOD

Eating in air-conditioned comfort

BOLLYWOOD!

Dance scene from the movie *Devdas*

Bollywood is the name of India's massive film and TV industry. It's based in Mumbai ('Bollywood' comes from the city's old name, Bombay). Every year hopeful young actors, singers and dancers arrive in Mumbai, dreaming that they will one day become big stars. For a very few, the dream comes true.

GOING TO THE CINEMA

If you want to go to see a film in India, you'll be joining in with one of the nation's most popular leisure activities. In the countryside, mobile cinemas showing the latest movies pitch up regularly, and are always busy. There are permanent cinemas in every town and city; modern multiplexes are most likely to have films subtitled in English.

> "I would love to work in a Bollywood film. There's so much drama and colour in the films there."
>
> — Brad Pitt, Hollywood star

PLAN A SUCCESSFUL BOLLYWOOD MOVIE

If you'd like to try writing your own Bollywood movie, remember that they often include key ingredients. This three-point plan should get you started:

1. Come up with a good story

The plots of Bollywood films often seem to include similar events:

- a kidnapping or two
- young people who are in love but whose parents disapprove
- corrupt politicians linked to local baddies
- long-lost relatives, especially brothers and sisters who have been separated by accident

2. Get a big star

Big stars such as Aishwarya Rai (sometimes called 'the most beautiful woman in India') and Shahrukh Khan always pull in the fans.

3. Add music and lots of dancing

Bollywood actors are sometimes called *paisa vasool*, which means 'money's worth'. It's because they don't only act, they also sing and dance. Most films include many singing and dancing sequences.

Bollywood gets everywhere – shooting a Bollywood movie in London

Bollywood publicity poster

FILM AND MUSIC

BEGINNER'S HINGLISH

Hinglish is just what it sounds like: a combination of Hindi and English. It is often used in Bollywood films. Here are a few beginner's words:

airdash:	go somewhere in a rush
stadium:	bald man with ring of remaining hair
pre-pone:	do something early (opposite of postpone)
glassy:	thirsty
timepass:	something that passes time
badmash:	badly behaved person

MUSIC IN INDIA

Music has always been an important part of life in India. You hear it at religious ceremonies, parties or just as the background noise of everyday life. Wander along a busy street and you might hear traditional music from various parts of India, modern film music, pop or hip-hop. Bands that mix Indian and Western styles are also popular.

Checking out the newest music releases

FREDDIE OR FARROKH?

Freddie Mercury of the rock band Queen was actually born Farrockh Bomi Bulsara. His parents were Indian, and he was brought up near Mumbai.

THE DEWARISTS

The Dewarists is a popular music TV series in India. Actress and singer Monica Dogra hosts the show.

In each episode, musicians from different areas, who normally play different types of music, visit a region of India. Sometimes the musicians even come from abroad. They work together to make new music, and the climax of each show is a performance of their new song.

Searching YouTube for 'The Dewarists' brings up clips of the songs.

TOP TASTER TRACKS

These songs are available on music-streaming websites, and Internet searches will also bring up videos.

1. Chickni Chameli

This song is from the hit 2012 movie *Agneepath*, which earned over a billion rupees within a month of release. The video has a great song-and-dance routine.

2. Ain't Nothing Like The Southside

(band: Machas With Attitude)

South Indian folk music mixed with hip-hop, from one of India's leading bands.

3. Maaya

(band: Mohut Chauhan with Indian Ocean)

Indian Ocean is one of the biggest acts in India, and Mohit Chauhan is one of the country's top singers.

4. Devil's Spoke

(band: Laura Marling, Mumford and Sons and Dharohar Project)

Traditional music from Rajasthan, in the northwest of India, blended with two of the world's biggest folk acts. This is as crazy as it sounds – but good, too.

FILM AND MUSIC

MUSIC FESTIVALS

If you're really into music, head for one of the festivals that take place around India in winter. The temperatures are cooler at this time of year, making it easier to jump up and down!

THE FIREFLIES FESTIVAL

To get to the Fireflies Festival, take a taxi from Bangalore to Dinnepalya. After 20 km of traffic, you reach the peace and quiet of one of the cutest festivals in India.

Once inside, head for the performance area. It is in a natural amphitheatre, in the shade of a banyan tree and next to a cool lake. Sit back and settle down to hear acts ranging from local musicians to singers from other countries.

HELPING THE ADIVASI

Adivasi are the original people of India, similar to Aborigines in Australia. They often live in poverty. The profits from the Fireflies Festival are used to help Adivasi children get an education.

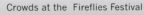
Crowds at the Fireflies Festival

TOP INDIAN MUSIC FESTIVALS

There are hundreds of music festivals and events in India each year. Here are locals' tips for four to try:

DECEMBER:

Sunburn, Goa

This electronic music festival is a big one, with over 100,000 people (and complaints from the locals about the traffic it causes). Sunburn is probably more popular with foreign visitors than Indians.

JANUARY:

Jaipur Literature Festival

Hang on, that says 'Literature Festival'. Yes, but in the evenings visitors huddle around bonfires in the grounds of the Diggi Palace and listen to all kinds of world music played in the open air.

FEBRUARY:

Storm, Coorg

Storm was India's first Glastonbury-style camping festival (and in 2011 it had to be cancelled because of heavy rain). It is one of the few where you can fall asleep in your tent listening to musicians playing around campfires.

OCTOBER:

Rajasthan International Folk Festival, Jodhpur

Traditional Rajasthan songs are about everyday things like planting crops and fetching water (the Thar Desert is nearby, and water is scarce). The festival takes place in the beautiful old Mehrangarh Fort, in the city of Jodhpur.

ADVENTURE SPORTS

Mountain biking in REAL mountains – the Himalayas

Most people know that India is great for mountaineers. In the far north are some of the world's highest mountains, including the third tallest anywhere, Kanchenjunga. What you might not realise is that India is a great place for all kinds of other adventure sports, too.

MANALI – ADVENTURE CENTRAL

One great place to head for if you're a thrill seeker is Manali. A Hindu story tells that mankind was reborn in this river valley, after a great flood had washed away the rest of the world. The town was once the start of an ancient trade route across the Himalayas that led all the way to China.

Today, Manali is known for its whitewater rafting and kayaking. The hiking and rock climbing are also fantastic in this area. In wintertime there is heli-skiing, snowboarding, ice climbing and mountaineering. When you're finally tired out, a 30-minute walk out of town will take you to the hot springs and a relaxing bath.

Rope crossing the rapids near Manali

SURFING INDIA

For surfers used to crowded beaches and cold water, India is a surfing paradise. There are hardly any surfers here, and the water is always warm. There are waves all year, with the surf at its biggest between May and September.

If you want to surf in India, remember that the ocean near towns and cities is often very polluted. The water is too dirty for surfing near Mumbai, for example.

A little bit of surf trivia: some people claim that the word 'surf' comes from the Indian word *suffe*, meaning coastline.

OTHER ADVENTURE TOWNS

1. Coorg – *(Karnataka State)*

From October to February, this is a popular area for trekking. You can also do whitewater rafting, rock climbing and fishing.

2. Rishikesh and Auli – *(Uttarakhandl State)*

Rishikesh, 'Gateway To The Himalayas', is a great place for trekking and whitewater rafting. In winter, a five-hour drive brings you to Auli, where there is good skiing and snowboarding.

Whitewater rafting on the River Ganges

SPORT AND LEISURE

INDIA – A CRICKET-CRAZY COUNTRY

Almost anywhere can be used as a cricket ground

S port is popular in India, and lots of people spend their leisure time watching or taking part. Indians like hockey (which used to be the most popular sport), football and tennis. But one sport is far more popular than any other: cricket.

FROM WASTE GROUND TO GRAND GROUNDS

Cricket is played and watched everywhere in India. Most pieces of open waste ground have a group of kids playing cricket on them. The kids are probably dreaming of one day playing somewhere very different: the giant grounds of the Indian Premier League (IPL), or even in the national team.

THE INDIAN PREMIER LEAGUE

The IPL might as well be called the WORLD Premier League, because it features just about all the world's best players. The games are Twenty20 cricket: they last about three hours, with lots of attacking play. If you haven't watched a match before, they are an exciting introduction to cricket.

CRICKET RIVALRIES

Indian cricket fans take all international matches seriously, but two opponents in particular get Indian cricketers and fans specially worked up.

1. India v Pakistan

The neighbouring countries have fought four wars since 1947. In fact, the first war started in 1947, just two months after the countries had been formed. No wonder their cricket matches get the fans excited.

2. India v England

The British ruled India for over 100 years and few Indians were pleased about it. Today there is a special pleasure in defeating England on the cricket pitch.

Chennai Super Kings batsman Murali Vijay

SPORT AND LEISURE

TOP CRICKET GROUNDS

Eden Gardens, Kolkata

(capacity 90,000; home IPL team Kolkata Knight Riders)

One of the oldest and biggest cricket grounds in India. Whether you're watching an IPL match or an international, there's always a great atmosphere.

Wankhede Stadium, Mumbai

(capacity 45,000; home IPL team Mumbai Indians)

Mumbai is the most cricket-crazy city in a cricket-mad country, and this is the main stadium for big matches.

MA Chidambaram Stadium, Chennai

(capacity 50,000; home IPL team Chennai Super Kings)

This is the ground where one of the earliest matches between India and England was played, in 1934. (Don't worry, the stadium has since been modernised.)

FREE TIME

Indians – especially young people, who are expected to study hard in their free time – value whatever leisure time they get. In the cities people spend free time socialising in ways most visitors will find familiar. The countryside is different, and here people are likely to be more traditional in how they behave.

The Amar Touring Cinema's truck in Palli

COUNTRYSIDE

If country people have free time, they often spend it at a local club. One thing you notice in the countryside is that men and women do not mix together as freely as in the cities. So for women, there will be clubs for sewing and crafts. Popular activities for men include cricket, football, snooker and billiards.

URBAN AREAS

Young Indians in urban areas spend their free time in similar ways to young people all around the world. They meet friends at the mall, eat out, and go to health clubs and the cinema. Men and women are more likely to socialise together than in the countryside, though they normally do this in groups rather than pairs.

KIDS

In India, getting a good education is seen as the key to future success. The school curriculum is demanding, so Indian kids are kept very busy with schoolwork. And because doing extra work earns students points towards a university place, many also learn an instrument, dance or learn a language in their free time.

Teenagers get together in a fruit-juice bar

PUSHKAR CAMEL FAIR

Each year, 50,000 camels (and their owners) arrive in Pushkar for a five-day fair. The highlight is the camel beauty parades. The camels are shaved, dressed up and decorated to make them look even prettier. Sideshows include musicians, acrobats, dancers and magicians.

CHESS

Everywhere you go in India you can find people playing chess. It's one of the country's most popular games. In fact, India is thought to be where chess was born. The game that developed into modern chess first appeared in northwest India in the 500s.

PUBLIC HOLIDAYS

There are only three public holidays in India:

26 January:	Republic Day
15 August:	Independence Day
2 October	Mahatma Gandhi's Birthday

Each state also has its own holidays, which depend on the religion and culture of the area.

SPORT AND LEISURE

RELIGIOUS SITES AND FESTIVALS

The Golden Temple in Amritsar, the Sikhs' holiest site

Everywhere you go in India, you see signs of religion. Painted cows cross the street or wander through a market helping themselves to the goods. There are beautiful, ornate temples, ceremonies being performed and holy men begging in the streets.

FESTIVALS AND CELEBRATIONS

Most religious festivals are Hindu, but there are also Muslim, Sikh and other religious festivals. Visitors are usually welcome to join the celebrating crowds. Watch out for dangerous situations, though: people are sometimes trampled at festivals if a large crowd panics for some reason.

VISITING RELIGIOUS SITES

These tips will help you avoid offending anyone while visiting religious sites.

- Take off your shoes and wash your feet if there is somewhere to do so.

- Men should not wear shorts and women should not have bare legs or arms.

- In Hindu temples, men may be asked to wear a *lungi*, a kind of kilt, and take off their shirt.

- In mosques and Sikh temples, female visitors should cover their head and shoulders with a scarf.

KUMBH MELA: THE WORLD'S BIGGEST FESTIVAL

Kumbh Mela is a Hindu festival, where people purify themselves in the waters of the holy river, the Ganges. It is held every three years, and is said to be the biggest human gathering on Earth. In 2013, over 100 million people are thought to have attended.

TOP RELIGIOUS FESTIVALS

There are hundreds of religious festivals in India every year – so many that it would be hard to visit India without seeing one. These are a few top picks, with places to see them.

DIWALI (OCT OR NOV):

Amritsar

Diwali is mainly a Hindu festival, but in Amritsar it is shared between Hindus, Sikhs, Jains and some Buddhists. The fireworks and lights over the famous Golden Temple are breathtaking.

HOLI (FEB OR MAR):

New Delhi

Holi celebrates the defeat and destruction of the evil demoness Holika. People spend the day smearing coloured powder on themselves, throwing it at others, and drenching themselves in water. It's particularly rowdy in New Delhi.

GANESH CHATURTHI (AUG OR SEPT):

Mumbai

Statues of Lord Ganesha, the elephant-headed Hindu god, are paraded through the streets. There is a lot of music and celebration, and in Mumbai, on the last day, the statues (apparently, over 150,000 of them) are taken for a swim.

KRISHNA JANMASHTAMI (AUG OR SEPT):

Mathura

This festival celebrates the Hindu god Lord Krishna's birth in the city of Mathura. Clay pots filled with butter, curd and money are strung from high buildings. Young people form human pyramids to try to get at them.

RELIGION

THE HIMALAYAS

At India's northern edge is one of the world's great mountain ranges, the Himalayas – sometimes called 'the roof of the world'. Life here is different from the crowded, hot lands below. In the highest regions winters and nights are cold, and there are far fewer people.

Snow being blown from the slopes of Kanchenjunga at sunrise

BORDER ARGUMENTS

In the Himalayas, India has border disputes with both Pakistan and China. They are arguing over who owns the territory of Jammu, Kashmir and Ladakh. Several wars have been fought as a result. The border is guarded on both sides.

TREKKING IN THE HIMALAYAS

If you want to explore the secret corners of the Indian Himalayas, you'll probably have to walk. High up in the mountains, many valleys are cut off by landslides or snow for much of the year. There are no cars, and few machines. It often takes hours even to reach the first village.

Trekking is hard work, but the effort is worthwhile. The paths from place to place go through rhododendron forest and across high-mountain pasture. On the way you see eagles, vultures and maybe – if you're really very lucky – a leopard.

A TREKKING DAY

What is a typical day's trekking like in the Indian Himalayas?

1. Start early – Pull on your boots and set off soon after dawn. The weather is often clearest early, so this is when you get the best views.

2. Do a long walk until lunchtime – Walking is usually most comfortable in the morning, before the day gets too hot. Many trekkers cover most of the day's distance before lunch.

3. Have a rest – Have lunch, then a rest in the shade, and perhaps even a little nap to get your energy back before carrying on.

4. Short walk to dinner – A shorter walk in the late afternoon should get you to your overnight stop, and perhaps some goat curry or fried chicken for dinner.

5. Stargazing, then bed – By now you'll just want to crawl into your sleeping bag. Before you do, have a look at the stars: they seem bigger and brighter here than anywhere else.

Bright stars on a clear Himalayan night

FRINGES OF INDIA

OFFSHORE ISLANDS

India has many offshore islands, but two main groups are popular with visitors. To the west, in the Indian Ocean, is Lakshadweep, 'The 100,000 Islands'. To the east of India, far out in the Bay of Bengal, are the Andaman and Nicobar islands.

Visitors cool down in a shallow lagoon, Lakshadweep islands

LAKSHADWEEP

Though there are said to be 100,000 islands in this coral-island archipelago, only 10 have people living on them full-time. The main industries are fishing and tourism. Visitors come mostly for the clean seas and water sports. Snorkelling and diving, windsurfing and sailing are all popular.

LAKSHADWEEP – RESTRICTED ACCESS

Everyone – Indian or visitor – has to have a government permit to visit Lakshadweep. Non-Indians are only allowed to stay on three of the islands. You get there from the mainland city of Kochi by boat or plane. The boat takes 14-18 hours, the plane 1.5 hours.

Mosque in Kavaratti, Lakshadweep

ANDAMAN AND NICOBAR

These islands are so far out in the Bay of Bengal that they are actually closer to Burma, on the other side, than India. Even so they have become a popular holiday destination for Indians and foreign visitors. They are famous for great snorkelling and diving. People also come to see historical sites such as Cellular Jail, the old British prison.

PRISONS AND EXILE

When the British ruled India, they used Andaman and Nicobar as a place to store 'troublemakers'. After an Indian uprising in 1857 they exiled about 200 people to the islands. In the 1900s, the British also put leading campaigners for Indian independence in prison there.

THE 2004 TSUNAMI

In 2004, the Indian Ocean was hit by a giant tsunami caused by an undersea earthquake. The Andaman and Nicobar Islands were badly affected. Over 2,000 people died and the ocean permanently flooded 123 km^2 of territory.

Few of the victims were from local native peoples. Their traditional stories warned them that if the sea level suddenly dropped, a giant wave was on its way. When the sea did suddenly drop on 26 December, they fled to safety on higher ground.

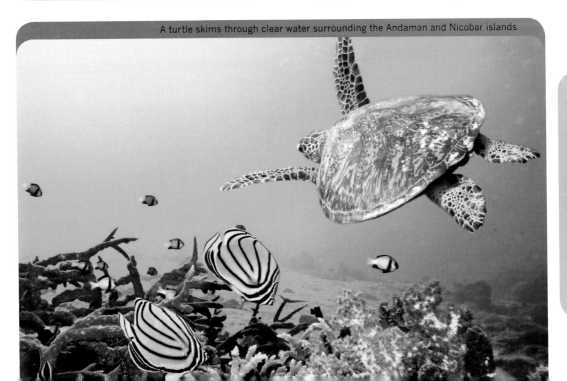
A turtle skims through clear water surrounding the Andaman and Nicobar islands

FRINGES OF INDIA

KEY INFORMATION FOR TRAVELLERS

LANGUAGE

Hindi is the most widely spoken language in India, with just fewer than half of the people speaking it as their main language. There are lots of other languages, so many people learn English as a second language, to be able to communicate with others.

ENTERING INDIA

Your passport must be valid for at least 180 days after your arrival in the country, or you won't be allowed in. Visitors from the EU, USA, Canada, Australia and New Zealand also need a visa.

HEALTH

If you are unlucky enough to get ill, healthcare is very good in towns and cities. It is expensive, though, and India does not have agreements with other countries to treat their citizens for free. Travel insurance is essential.

The biggest health risk in India is probably the water, which is likely to cause diarrhoea or worse if you drink it, or even if you eat food that has been washed in it.

These tips will help you stay well:

• Only use bottled water for drinking, brushing teeth, and washing your face. Always check the seal on the bottled water to make sure it has not been opened and refilled. If you can't get bottled water, boil any water before use. Don't eat salad or other uncooked food that could have been washed in water, or have ice in drinks.

• Do not drink milk unless it has been boiled, or eat dairy foods such as cheese.

• Only eat food that has been thoroughly cooked, particularly meat.

In some areas, mosquitoes spread dengue fever and malaria, both very serious diseases. Take great care to avoid being bitten.

Check the meat is cooked and avoid the salad

POSTAL SERVICES

The national post service is called India Post. Post offices in towns and cities are usually open Monday to Saturday 10:00–13:00 and 13:30–16:30 in towns and cities.

Letters and parcels take anything from a day to a week or more to arrive within India. Airmail to Europe, North America or Australia takes about two weeks.

MOBILE NETWORKS

Use of mobile phones, including smartphones, is growing rapidly in India. The coverage is good in towns and cities, but in rural and isolated areas there probably won't be any coverage at all. 3G is not always available.

Although roaming on your home contract is possible, using a foreign phone is expensive, especially for data: make sure you turn off data roaming. Indian SIMs to use while in the country are not expensive.

INTERNET PROVISION

In bigger towns and cities, Internet access is generally good. There are Internet cafés in most tourist hotspots, and an increasing number of hotels have Wifi. In remote rural areas, Internet access may not be as easy to find.

Going online at an Internet cafe

STAYING SAFE

Indian people are generally kind and welcoming. However, crime against visitors can be a problem. These tips will help you to stay safe.

- Never wear expensive watches or jewellery in public, or show that you have large amounts of cash.

- Avoid letting people see you have high-cost electronic goods such as mobile phones.

- Women should avoid going out alone, especially at night, unless they are in a very safe, busy area. It is a good idea to wear loose clothes that cover your arms and legs: tight clothes and bare flesh are seen as immodest.

- Never accept lifts from people you do not know well, and always be wary of situations where you may find yourself alone with strangers.

CURRENCY:

Indian rupees, symbol IRP or Rs (€1=Rs75, £1=Rs85, $1=Rs55). ATM cash withdrawal is possible in towns and cities, where bank cards are also often accepted. You can get local money at banks, airports and official moneychangers.

TELEPHONE DIALLING CODES:

To call India from outside the country, add the exit code from your country (from the UK this is 00), add 91 to the beginning of the number, and drop the zero from the city code.

To call another country from India, add 00 and the country code of the place you are dialling to the beginning of the number, and drop the zero.

International phone cards can be bought before your trip, or while in India.

TIME ZONE:

Unlike other large countries, India has only one time zone, Indian Standard Time (IST). (There used to be two time zones, with Bombay Time 39 minutes behind the rest of the country, but this finished in 1955.) IST is 5.5 hours ahead of Greenwich Mean Time.

OPENING HOURS:

Most businesses are open 09:00–19:00 Monday to Saturday, and close on Sunday. Some stores also open on Sundays, especially in big cities, where they may also stay open much later than 19:00.

HOW TO BEHAVE:

Greetings: when you meet someone, the usual way to say hello is *namaste*. Men often shake hands, but women may prefer not to. Using someone's first name without being invited risks rudeness. It's better to use Mr, Mrs or Miss and then the person's surname.

AS A GUEST:

If you're lucky enough to be invited to someone's home, it's good manners to arrive about 30 minutes late, and to remove your shoes as you go in. Dinner guests often bring a gift, such as chocolates or flowers. Most people eat with their fingers – it's important to use only your right hand, even if you are left-handed. Never thank your hosts for dinner, which is thought rude and unfriendly. Instead, make a point of saying how good the food was and how much you enjoyed it.

FINDING OUT MORE

BOOKS TO READ: NON-FICTION

Countries in Our World: India Darryl Humble (Franklin Watts, 2013)
Informative, fact-packed guide to India.

Mumbai Jen Green (Evans Brothers, 2007)
This book contains information on how Mumbai is changing, its neighbourhoods, environmental concerns, and much more.

Slumgirl Dreaming: Rubina's Journey To The Stars Rubina Ali (Delacorte Books, 2009)

Rubina Ali grew up in the slums of Mumbai, but her life changed forever when she got the part of Latika in the hit movie *Slumdog Millionaire*. This is her story so far.

BOOKS TO READ: FICTION

Boys Without Names Kashmira Sheth (HarperCollins, 2010)
Gopal is 11 when his family leaves their village in the countryside. They move to Mumbai in search of a better life. But then Gopal's father goes missing, and Gopal himself is imprisoned in a sweatshop. This is the story of what happens next.

The Conch Bearer Chitra Banerjee Divakaruni (Aladdin, 2003)
Twelve-year-old Anand lives in Kolkata and works in a tea shop. One day, he is entrusted with an important mission. Anand must help return a magical conch shell to the secret valley in the Himalayas from which it has been stolen. His adventures have just begun.

Climbing the Stairs Padma Venkatraman (Penguin, 2008)
Set in British-ruled India during the Second World War, this is the story of 15-year-old Vidya. She hopes one day to go to university, but then after a family tragedy she and her brother are forced to move in with their relatives – who believe women should be married, not educated...

WEBSITES:

http://www.incredibleindia.org
This is the official tourist guide to India. It's not 100% straightforward to navigate, but it is packed with useful information. The 'Essentials' tab takes you to lots of practical information about India, while clicking on 'Discover' leads to information on the country's history, geography and culture. There are also clickable maps under 'Travel' that allow you to explore the different regions.

http://tinyurl.com/ypn8hx
This link will take you to the CIA (Central Intelligence Agency) web page about India. It's quite dry, but crammed full of useful information and statistics.

Note to parents and teachers:
Every effort has been made by the Publishers to ensure that these websites are suitable for children, that they are of the highest educational value, and that they contain no inappropriate or offensive material. However, because of the nature of the Internet, it is impossible to guarantee that the contents of these sites will not be altered. We strongly advise that Internet access is supervised by a responsible adult.

THE ESSENTIALS

INDEX

Adivasi 28
Agra 7, 8, 21
Andaman and Nicobar
  (islands) 40, 41
auto-rickshaws 6, 16

Bangalore 7, 8, 11, 17,
  21, 28
bazaars 6, 7, 14, 18–19
beaches 6, 7, 8, 14, 31,
  40, 41
Bollywood 6, 24–25
Bombay see Mumbai
buses 17

caste (system) 10
Chandni Chowk 18
Chennai 8, 11, 17, 19,
  21, 33
chess 35
cinema 6, 24–25, 34
climate 9
climbing 8, 30
Coorg 6, 29, 31
cricket 7, 32–33, 34
currency 44

diving 40–41
Diwali 37

education 11, 12, 28, 34

festivals 6, 7, 10, 12, 15,
  28–29, 36–37
films 6, 24–25, 26, 27
Fireflies Festival 28
food 7, 13, 18, 20–23, 42

Ganesh Chaturthi 37
Ganges 7, 8, 9, 31, 36
Goa 7, 8, 16, 21, 29
Golden Temple 36, 37

Hampi 15
health/healthcare 23, 42
Himalayas 7, 8, 9, 30, 31,
  38–39

Hinduism/Hindus 10, 11,
  12, 15, 30, 36, 37
Hinglish 6, 25
Holi 7, 10, 15, 37
holidays, public 35
housing 8, 11

independence 9, 33
Indian Premier League
  32, 33
inequality 8, 10, 11, 13,
  28
islands, offshore 40–41

Jaipur 7, 8, 17, 19, 21,
  29
Jodhpur 29

Kanchenjunga 8, 9, 30, 38
Kolkata 8, 11, 15, 17, 19,
  21, 33
Krishna Janmashtami 37
Kumbh Mela 36

Lakshadweep (islands) 6,
  40
landscape 8–9
languages 10, 11, 25, 42

Manali 30
maps 8, 21
markets see bazaars
Mattu Pongal 12
Mercury, Freddie 26
monsoon 9
mountains 6, 7, 8, 9, 14,
  30–31, 38, 39
mountain sports 30–31
Mumbai 6, 7, 8, 11, 13,
  14–15, 19, 21, 22, 24,
  26, 31, 33, 37
music 6, 7, 24, 26–29,
  34, 37
festivals 6, 28–29

New Delhi/Old Delhi 7, 8,
  9, 11, 15, 17, 18, 21,
  37

Pakistan 8, 9, 33, 38
palaces 6, 7, 15
people 10–11, 28, 41
phones 43
population 11
post (postal service) 43
Pushkar Camel Fair 35

Rajasthan International
Folk Festival 29
religion 7, 10, 11, 12, 15,
  26, 35, 36–37

safety, personal 11, 17,
  43
shopping 6, 12, 14,
  18–19
snacks 6, 20, 22–23
snorkelling 40, 41
socialising 34
sport 7, 30–33, 40, 41
  adventure sports
  30–31, 40
Storm Music Festival 6,
  29
Sunburn (festival) 29
surfing 31

television 24, 26
temples 7, 8, 36
Thar Desert 8, 29
The Dewarists 26
tsunami (2004) 41
trains 16, 17
transport 6, 16–17
trekking 7, 8, 30, 31, 38,
  39

Udaipur 15

Varanasi 7, 8, 21

wars 9, 33, 38
wildlife 38, 41